A Walk Through My

Mind

Writings by

Dennis M. Stanfield

Copyright Page

ISBN: 978-0-6151-5246-2

© 2007 Dennis M. Stanfield

Dedication

This book is dedicated to my late grandfather, Tommie Lee Stanfield, Sr. Also my great grandfather, William Childress, and the rest of my family and close friends. I am because all of you are! And to anyone who may need a laugh, inspiration, a vent or just to say, "I know what you mean." This is for you also. You all are my inspirations!

Introduction

A Walk Through My Mind came about from my best friend and other friends telling me to seriously consider publishing my writings. My writings, like feelings, have a wide range, although personal. So hopefully you as a reader can feel the writings and take something away from them. I was inspired by everything. By God, my family, friends, music, politics and life itself. I pray everyone reading this book will enjoy it.

God bless and let's get it…

Table of Contents

Title Page	1
Copyright Page	2
Dedication Page	3
Introduction	4
Table of Contents	5
Part 1: Love	7
4 Letter Word	8
What If	9
Déjà vu	10
She's In God	11
Portrait of a Woman	12
In My Own Words	13
Cold Blooded	14
I Wanna Kno	15
Love Dream	16
Full Circle	17
Two Minutes	18
Loving Love	19
Untitled	20
Portraits of Women	21
Part 2: God	22
Smile	23
Never Leave Home With Out It	24
Big Homie	25
OpenMind	26
Soul Of a Man	27
Random	28
Don't Blame God	29
The Plan	30
Follow Me	31
Part 3: Creative	32
LIFE	33
Fiend	34
Let Me Holla	35
Food	36
Final Goodbye	37
Playa	38
Still a Playa	39
The Man	40
The Flyest	41
Seduction	42
Glamorous	43
Wings of B	44

© 2007 Dennis M. Stanfield

Just a Poem	45
Home	46
Part 4: Stories	47
My Mind	48
Diamond Rose	49
Play'd	50
Unknown	51
The Well	52
I Don't Know You	53
The Fight	54
Choice	55
American Dream	56
Roses	57
Part 5: Political/Social	58
Pro Black	59
Still Pro Black	60
Y'all Don't Hear Me	61
Paint Brush	62
Mental Stimulation	63
Leader	64
Dream Come Tru	65
Around My Way	66
Part 6: Personal	67
If and Might	68
Where I Stand	69
Spaceship	70
The Nice Guy Box	71
To Whom It May Concern	72
Questions	73
Void	74
I Live Down Here	75
1980 Sumin	76
Thank You	77
Thank You Page	78

Part 1

LVE

4 Letter Word

Love is a short but powerful word
Love can mean so much to a person
Love is more than an emotion
Love can become physical
Love is not just a state of mind
Love with the right person can be the best feeling ever
Love is not soft
Love can bring the Man out of the boy,
The Woman out of the girl
Where can you find love?
Love is tricky
Loving some one is different from being in Love with them
Love is like believing in God,
When you know…you know
And God doesn't lie
Love can be hard to find
Love from God can be found in the last place you would look
Love is easy to fall into but hard to maintain,
But any thing you want you'll have to work hard for
Love is worth fighting for
So don't Fall into love,
Rather Step into it and know what you want out of it
Love has no boundaries, no limits
Love is no race, color or religion
Love is next door,
Its long distance
It's right under your nose
Love has to be released and believed in
Blocking love is like blocking your blessing
Love = Respect + Trust + Friendship
Love your family and friends
Give love a try because you don't want to miss what Love offers

What If

What if I told you I loved you?
Would you believe me?
Or would you think of me as just another dude?
What if I told you I wasn't like them?
What if I told you I would respect and cherish you?
Try to make your dreams come true and fulfill your fantasies
What if I told you I'd never cheat on you?
I know you heard it before, but what if?
What if I told you I'd never put the hands to you?
Never to hit you but only to comfort you
What if I told you I'd always be there?
Where is there? Where ever you are
What if I told you I'm a strong black man?
A real one, not like the stereotype
What if I told you I wanted you to be independent?
I want you to think for your self and have your own mind
You might not believe me because men fear those women
What if I lied? Made one mistake?
Would you love me enough to forgive?
What if I ask for trust?
Would you give it to me? Could you give it to me?
What if I told you, you were 1st in my life?
Only behind God, would you believe that?
What if I wanted you to have our kids?
What if I told you I'd be a real dad, a real father?
You've seen enough men, would you trust me then?
What if I wanted to show you the world?
What if I wanted you to be mine forever?
Would you take that chance and take my hand?
What if I told you I loved you?
I know you heard it before, but what if?

Deja Vu

I see her every where I turn my head
She's the best thing since sliced bread
To sexy for herself like Right Said Fred
Wake up in the morning I feel her presence
Maybe because she's an Angel from heaven
Never seen her before
But I think I like her like a metaphor
Ha-ha Lupe good looking out
The love we have will fade that I doubt
Turnaround, I thought I saw her
Man, how can I describe her?
She's miles away but I see her kind of like a star
She like my best friend and my homie
With out her, I can be in a crowd and feel lonely
Her voice takes me to a place I've never been
But how can it be déjà vu if I've never been
Think, come on Den
The idea had me loosing my mind
But maybe because my Angels been here all this time

She's In God

I've heard that a woman's heart should be hidden in God
So hidden that to find her, he must seek God
So in seeking God, he would be seeking perfection
Like a renewal of love or resurrection
That's the only way to find true love
Who better than God to seek for love?
If she is in Him and he's in Him
No one can break the bond of them
How could he pass that up after seeking so hard through the soul?
He can't if forever with her is his goal
And forever with Him involved is called eternal
And through His love he could be happy in a urinal
But her heart is so pure
Their love is so strong it will always endure
They're so deep rooted in God that any problem has a cure
She's in God, imbedded deep
And at night that helps him sleep

Portrait Of a Woman

Eyes bright as the sun
Just look into her eyes and see she is the one
Hair a nice brown like the softest sands
My heart around her beats like a Southern band
Smile lights up the sky like the 4th of July
Let her go never would I
Skin is the color of coco butter
Man she got a hold of a brother
Body that of a Greek Goddess
Nothing else to say but...Goddess
She is strong in mind, body, spirit and soul
God has sent his Angel and to protect her is my goal
This portrait hangs not on a wall but in my heart
So that way my view of her will never part
This is a portrait of a woman
Matter fact, a portrait of my woman

In My Own Words

This is how it went down back then
She came into my life like a world wind
It happen so fast and ended even faster
I felt like I was used by Napster
Because she downloaded instead of buying the real copy
She caught me on the rebound so my game was sloppy
She penetrated my defenses easy
Had me going crazy like Jeezy
Thought I was done falling hard, guess not
I fell again and got, got
Now I'm on an emotional roller coaster
It looks good like a new poster
When I'm up I'm up and when I'm down I'm down
My heart is in the lost and found
When you've loved and lost so many times
The question of love is silent like a mime
Too many questions get in the way
You'll be feeling two different ways in one day
I want to give my heart freely but the hill is tall
I'm thinking with my mind till my heart thaws
Trying to figure out what's the cause
In my own words from then till now
Don't know if I've totally recovered even though she's like wow
Yeah I'm ready right
But I'm still being pulled back like a kite
I can't pull away from something man
It's not a person or a thing, but the balls in my hand
I feel like I'm a fumble it
It's not her fault I feel like this
I can't move on because of bull and its killing me
I'm singing the blues like King BB
I see I have a problem of getting close and pulling back
Because I don't want to feel pain like that
Pain of the past may hurt my future plans
I dived in fast and took a chance
Now I got to think realistically about it all
These rushed decisions can lead to a hard fall
Man, I'm messed up
Like sounds that don't bump
Well, Just my thoughts in my own words

© 2007 Dennis M. Stanfield

Cold Blooded

Yo you seen Troy
You seen what chick did to ol' boy
Started a war between two countries
You mess up with me you only got once B
Because I'm not gone be hurt like that
Now a days fallen in love is fallen to a trap
Call me cold blooded but Cleopatra brought down Rome
And I'll be damned if she brings down my home
To win and loose love is a part of life
No three strikes, you got less than twice
Its probably wrong going in thinking the worst
But hurting again could make my heart burst
It don't mean I'm a playa or I've lost respect
I respect you enough to say don't loose rest
Just so you don't get it confused
I've lost nothing, still not one of those dudes
Call it what you want
I'm too old for games and trying to stunt
It is what it is, be blunt

I Wanna Know

I wanna know what makes you smile
I wanna know what makes you laugh
I wanna know everyday how ya day was
I wanna know what makes you cry
I wanna know your fears
    So we can face them together
I wanna know your goals
    So that I can help you achieve them
I wanna know things you don't want to tell me
    But that time of the month stuff, I'll pass
I wanna know your views beliefs and morals
I wanna know why?
I wanna know everyday that you love me
I wanna know why I'm different
I wanna know why you're different
I wanna know what you like and dislike
I wanna know if that feels good or not
I wanna know why you're hurt or sad
    So I can never make the same mistake twice
I wanna know all about YOU
I wanna know why you want to spend your life with me
I wanna know love
Why? Because I want to know

Love Dream

I saw the most beautiful silhouette
And in my mind her name I kept
I built the nerve to ask for her hand
And in circles we danced
As we danced we swayed like trees in the breeze
Stay with me forever was my plea
We danced then heard a beat with a hop
And we followed to take a long walk with Jill Scott
Amazing the sun went down but never turned to night
Hey it's a dream right
We hugged and kissed
I saw heaven every time I touched her lips
Floating above the clouds, that's where we are now
To be realistic I don't want to come down
Me and my sexy love locked inside like the Ne-Yo way
Sorry Mr. Stanfield is out of the office for the day
This dream seems like a lifetime
But really I didn't make it past halftime
I know the girl in my dreams
The one who has my heart on a string
I woke up to a silhouette of you
And to a dream come true

Full Circle

Start at one point come back later
Going 360°, hey there
Didn't really think I'd come full circle
But even ol' girl got a 2nd chance in the Color Purple
Coming back around even though always in front of me
Why did it take a full circle for me to see
Now my feelings a full circle have they come
The indifference beats my heart like a drum
To come full circle my feelings had to grow and mature
And now this full circle makes me want to be yours

Two Minutes

In Two Minutes just thinking of you can change my day
You make me feel good in every way
Not worried about the cares of the world
So in a daze I could trip over a simple cord
But I know you'll be there to catch me
I hope you think, what would life be with out me
Two Minutes in front of you, I feel corny saying it
But I wouldn't even think of trading it
Finally I'm at peace
All the indecision can cease
A Two Minute hug in her arms is like a lifetime
That feeling is one of a kind
Don't rush but in Two Minutes I said yes to forever
Just need a good way to ask, something clever
Two Minutes can be a long time but I need more than two
Because Two Minutes isn't enough time to tell how much I love you
But all I got is Two Minutes to get to forever with you
And forever is the icing on an already wonderful cake called you

Loving Love

I love Love
I love everything about Love
I love to Love
And for Love to love me
I love the joy in Love
      She's always so wonderful
I love the smile of Love
I love Love's eyes
      Love knows my soul
My Love is different
My Love is mine
Yeah everyone has love
      But no one has my Love
And everyone knows I love Love
Because you can't hide
Love knows
So be real with Love
Because Love may not work out
      But Love will always love
I love Love

Untitled

Night falls like a cover over a scared kids eyes
Rain pours like grieving mothers eyes
Sadness now but joy comes in the morn
Like a new start, kind of like being reborn
Another chance to make things right
That loving feeling gets me high as a kite
Happy endings only happen to movie people
So look at it like this my second chance is the sequel
Will I make it right will I succeed?
I'm praying so I hope its my destiny
Her love is hard to get rid of like the dirt under your nails
Be good to her she'll be behind you like an animals tail
That good love like you were locked up in jail
Yeah she'll stick around like hair gel
So now the sun rises on a new day and chapter
I'll make this last long like a bomb from Travis Hafner
Now I'm a be the guy that gets the chick
And ride off like a hero at the end of the flick

Portraits Of Women

These are portraits of women that mean a lot to me
With out them I probably wouldn't be
Through God this woman gave me life
She inspires me to sore to new heights
Her words are soft and subtle yet powerful
Everything she does is so meaningful
She is my best friend and super mom
When the seas are raging she makes them calm
She is my doctor, lawyer, and counselor with out fee
I wouldn't know what to do if she wasn't here with me

What can I say but pink and green?
She has the sweetest smile but she can be mean
Ha-ha she'll kill me for that but hey
What are best friends for but to brighten each others day
She always leaves me with a smile
We can't go out late any more because she is wild
When we are sleepy we act a fool
That's why I love her, she is so cool
I know she'll always be there so I'm not worried
I just hope she knows I'm her friend till our vision gets blurry

Now this next lady is kind of tough
What we went through was kind of rough
What is said is said and done is done
I always cared for her from day one
We may not agree on what's ahead
But I always say a prayer for her before I go to bed
She is growing into a woman and learning what life's about
Sometimes it's like swimming up stream and your a trout
We'll always be close because of our past
But it wont stop there because our friendship will last
But these women contributed to my life in a major way
And this is one way I can pay them back with out actual pay
So if you got women in your life treat them right
BESIDE every good man is a good woman and for you they'll fight

© 2007 Dennis M. Stanfield

Part 2

GOD

Smile

Smile is an expression of joy & happiness
Smile is not a sign of weakness
      Mean mugs are not always needed
Smile whenever possible
Smile is a sign of comfort
Smile in the moments that make you laugh and cry
Smile in the face of danger and stress
Smile because the sun shines through the rain clouds
Smile when you don't feel like it because you never know who likes your smile
Smile with your family because they know when your down
Smile is strength
Smile could pick up another's frown, heart and spirit
Smile is simple
Smile because God smiles on us all

© 2007 Dennis M. Stanfield

Never Leave Home With Out It

Never leave home with out it
And "it" being the Spirit
And the Spirit being God
And God being the reason I have breath
So why would I leave home with out Him?
Makes no sense right?
Good thing David left with God, huh?
Man, what if I left "It" at home?
I might not have made it on the freeway
That test might as well have been in German
And oh when that pretty girl walked by
That could've been trouble
Everything happens for a reason
And I don't know the future
But I know Someone who does
So why would I leave home with out Him?

Big Homie

Sun shines through the clouds as the rain dries
See there is a brighter day on the other side
Yesterday seemed as though it would never end
D'evils was trying break me but I would only bend
The Father in the sky got my back
So I really shouldn't have to worry bout jack
Easy concept but reality is tough
But what He went through was pretty rough
So I must remember He'll never give me anything I can't handle
Now I can sit in the pocket, I don't have to scramble
These thoughts get my day started
Turn on the news and a storm is charted
It's cool because I through my armor on
And my big Homie from up stairs is going where I'm going
Put my smile on and stand tall
Said it before God smiles on us all
Get in the car, not too much but the base does humm
Man, soon as I'm out the house the clouds come
Hey son do you know what I'm stopping you foo (for)?
Because I'm young and I'm black and my hats real low
D'evils but I brush it off my shoulder
I'm good long as the piece stays in the holster
He leaves I see the sun start to break
What's up with the traffic? I'm in a rush, I'm late
Turn my Jay-Z down not up
Oh my God it's like a five car pile up
The sun breaks all the way through
Big Homie whispers, that could've been you!
Now I kind of thank the cop for stopping my whip
Because that could've been my car that flipped
Yo when it's dark and the clouds is out
Big Homie up stairs got your back no doubt

© 2007 Dennis M. Stanfield

OpenMind

We should be like green leaves, know why?
Because they grow until the day they die
Life is longer then you think
But it can be quick as a blink
This concept to understand can be hard B
Like describing colors to a man who can't see
You can be a real man and hard and still respect women
But seeing my young brothers today is sour like a lemon
They think they keeping it real so they rebel
But it looks like an episode of Dave Chappelle
When keeping it real goes wrong
That'll get you lost like a needle in a haystack
Know what you fighting for, don't be a solider in Iraq
Today's leaders can and will lead you on a wrong path
Tell you you're free to run but cut your calf
Now we're limping through this long race
But we don't help each other, rather knock the next man to quicken our pace
Open your mind to my way of thinking
Seems the government is playing games while I'm blinking
But I can't let the world bring me down
So I find joy in the Man who wears a crown
My best friend keeps me laughing
Some of my boy's comments are just baffling
I'm not happy with the world but I love life
My friends and family help me enjoy life
Believe in God and keep an open mind
God won't lead you wrong, He's one of a kind

Soul Of a Man

Soul of a man is strong
But many strong souls are gone
My strong soul comes from a woman
Who put it in me to be a true man
I do not control my soul, it controls me
But I can get in my own way and mess up what's to be
My soul has found another and strong soul has she
Now our souls have to get through good and tough times
Life isn't simple like these corny rap lines
The world will test my manhood, my soul
But me and my soul work for a higher goal
We use God as our pole
And we pole vault over that hole
If the soul of a man is strong, the mind and body can follow
Because the soul follows God, and Big Homie knows tomorrow
Your soul is not only what you think or what you do
But how you see life, your view
You can be the strongest and the hardest
But that wont necessarily get you he farthest
Your soul also reflects the past
Your ancestors, family, memories that last
What defines the soul of a man?
The willingness to always say "I can"
Through my eyes you can see my soul wears a shirt that says "I can"
I can do all things through Him
I can do big things for them
And by my side stands her
I'm ready for the world; my soul just had a rebirth
The soul of this man rises from the dirt

© 2007 Dennis M. Stanfield

Random

Well I'm just at my computer thinking
Ready to put down some random thoughts
Funny how quickly a good day can change
One little thing hits you the wrong way and that good feeling is gone
Doesn't even have to be a big deal
Someone did something or said something
The devil jumps all over that
Pushing you to take out anger on people
But it isn't worth wasting time and energy
Just be easy and keep to your self
But its like a chip on your shoulder
Then that leads to another
Now you got two problems on your hands
Frustrated with life
Well, can't really say that
I'm alive and in pretty good health
It's people out there in a worse position than me
But a mountain for you may not be that for someone else
No one knows your pain like…you
But its good to have friends around that keep you up
Also new ones that make you laugh in the weirdest ways
Keep positive people around and your frustrations won't seem as bad
Be real with God, he won't give you more than you could handle
Seems like all the bills are coming together at one time
But God blesses you in the slightest way to manage
Now there is nothing to complain about
What were you worried for?
Just go along with the game plan
This coach has never lost a game
And it's like MJ or Tom Brady in the clutch
But now that everything is ok and you wonder
You wonder how did you ever doubt God?
Instead of concentrating on things that you could handle and control
You worried bout things that God had a plan for
Plans that were really out of your control from jump
Well I guess I've done enough rambling
Stay blessed and believe you have a purpose

Don't Blame God

So you the man huh?
Walk by and laugh at the bums
You got your destiny in your own hands
You mapped it out and rolling out to your own plans
God is an after thought
You don't believe your soul was bought
You just living the life, the player way
Couple different ladies every other day
Leaving your wife and baby boy at home
You messed with the wrong girl and her man almost put one in ya dome
Only way you made it was the grace of God
And your wife and momma prayed so hard
You mine as well get it while you can
This makes you feel like a real man?
You got it good because she won't leave
Only because she don't want to do that to her seed
You think you got game and your supafly
But what you gone do when that lady says bye bye
And when you came home with a positive test
You made it easy on her, and put her wondering mind to rest
Now you blaming God, asking why he left
He gave you signs to change, but you needed to be hit in the chest
You turned your back on God
Now you're empty like no iTunes in the iPod
Your own selfish pride, don't blame God

© 2007 Dennis M. Stanfield

The Plan

Well what do you want out of life?
Let's start by 1st saying its not your life
You didn't create you
So to decide that, who are you?
You can't, you can only live
You float down stream like a twig
But wait, God has a plan to follow
You can't think about it, pretend your head is hollow
God's plan is better than yours will ever be
Read your Bible, you don't have to believe me
Wonder why your so stressed?
Wonder why your so down and depressed?
Nothings going right?
Man, I've been on that flight
Problems come in heavy light rain drops
And that's when you call on the one who can be called Pops
Me myself I struggle with the unknown
Trying to keep my faith but sometime it gets blown
I'm just trying to stay out of my own way
And let God lead my way
What I want out of life is to live
And for the people around me to live
God has a plan for you
Just be easy and let Him show you

Follow Me

Follow me to a world with out pain and sorrow
A place where the sunsets are long and today is tomorrow
Where a Being sits top a throne as King of Kings
And His servants have the most beautiful wings
They say it's like a land flowing with milk and honey
No cares of this world, no need for money
The walk ways are paved with gold
Everyone can have a royal robe
No disease or war or even fear
Right beside you are the ones you hold dear
And the Man on the throne is always near
Follow me to this place your soul is looking for
It'll be just like coming home, walking through that door
This place is not for all though, but all are welcome
Be dressed like a star or even a bum
Only evaluation is ya heart
And how much of it is Big Homie's part
Follow me to this place that is beyond belief
Dude right there, used to be a thief
Him, he never listened to his peeps
That lady sold her child for a hit
Then got paid to let dudes hit it
But they all realized enough was enough
They were weak but now they're tough
And it wasn't for chance or luck
We were all chosen ones like LeBron
Following a trail to which we are drawn
Searching for home with that third eye
Soon as you're born, your living to die
Don't worry about what you can or can't control
You just focus on your path and road
For one reason or another people in our lives come and go
But follow me to this place, where He wants to go
Matter fact don't follow me, follow Him

© 2007 Dennis M. Stanfield

Part 3

CREATIVE

LIFE

Life is what you make it they say
It's not the amount of breathes you take but the times that take your breath away
Forever is not promised so you must live
Everyday you must wake up like it's on purpose
Live in every moment because it could be worse
It could be your last
Find the one who makes you happy
Easier said then done
Life is about taking chances, learning from your mistakes
Its better to have loved and lost then never to have loved at all they say
Funny, when you loose that love it doesn't always seem that easy
Eventually when you look back, it was worth it
Life will show you ups and downs, sunshine and darkness
I haven't seen it all and I don't have the answers but I have my own experiences
Family above all is the most important thing in life
Even life knows that
LIFE is what you make it they say, make it yours

Fiend

You love the fast money and girls
Dodging bullets, hey this is your world
Chasing the American Dream
Best way you can trying to get that CREAM
Because Cash Rules
And here are your tools
Water, baking soda, pots and pans
All black gloves to cover your hands
Get respect or take it with a mean mug frown
You run this, get down or lay down
You cook up the product and feed the fiends
You take whatever they got, don't have to be green
You love the block and the rush
No love for chicks because the block is your crush
With a gat in your hand
You feel you the man
So deep in you couldn't leave if you wanted to
You're so blind to what's become of you
You rather die enormous than live dormant
But now you can't sleep, you live in torment
Hustling so hard you haven't heard a word
Now you've become addicted like fiends you serve
You hooked and won't give up the game
You're a fiend like them, now who is the lame?

Let Me Holla

You ever seen a Jamaican sunrise?
Walk on a beach with out a cloud in the sky?
House on the hill looks over clear blue sea
Go by private jet to anywhere you want to be
Go see Prague and have dinner in Italy
Lets fly to Egypt and check the pyramids
Next is Africa to check our heritage
Lets see some real lions, not the ones in the zoo
Don't get scared now, I'm talking to you
Diamonds? You want them you got them all
Cars? We gone ball till we fall
Listen here baby I'm a change the life
Stop messing around so I can call you wife
You'll be so fly famous chicks will be jealous
They'll be mad because they aren't us
Leave these lames alone and roll with a winner
Trust me I'm no beginner
What? Where is my jet?
Oh, I don't got it all yet
Give me a couple years those dreams will come true
What…well holla when they do?
Damn…

Food

Look at her looking like a fudge brownie
She so sexy, being away from her is haunting me
Deep chocolate skin, almond eyes
Fruit flavored lip gloss that never dries
Still taste it on my lips from her good byes
Stacked like a triple thick milk shake
Fresh scent like brownies I had her bake
Layered nice like ya favorite burger
Her love is all on me like pancakes with syrup all over
When she get it going she like hot wings
But she can be basic like boxed things
She sweet and healthy too
That's good for me because I have a sweet tooth
Melt in ya mouth and not ya hand, duh
Yeah she got a little M&M in her blood
And chocolate is my weakness
Greedy she makes me, but under control I have to keep this
But she loves to feed me
And I'm not worried, I'll be skinny till 53
Her ingredients make her the best for a good deal
And trust me, I never miss a good meal

Final Goodbye

Goodbyes are always hard to handle
I'm holding all this emotion in like water in a camel
You looking at me funny but you got to go
You know I love you but if my girl sees you a fit she'll throw
Hide you? But she ain't that slow
Besides she got people on her side
So don't make this harder than it has to be, goodbye
We had great times, but you're not good for me anymore
Love you always I will but I have to close and lock that door
You are soo sweet
Great times every time we would meet
But they say so sweet you'll make my teeth rot
Don't worry, like Luda you'll have my #1 spot
It just has to be this way
Maybe in another life, another day
I want you bad but I can't give in
And cheating on my wife is a sin
Even if it is just with ice cream, cakes and other sweets
LOL

Playa

Girl I'm a playa I thought you knew?
I'm sorry to hurt you but I'm a make it do what it do
I'm not a playa because I want to be
But because I have to be
You don't know what it's like being the nice guy
Getting taken advantage of, asking myself why?
See some girls don't know how to act when I treat them right
So used to the wrong man they waiting for a fight
If I can't spend money on her I have no hope
Yeah she ain't a gold digga just don't want a broke broke
It's not all girls fault I've closed up my heart
It's only a few but that makes up a big part
I'll still treat girls with respect
But a long relationship don't expect
One day I'll open up one day I'll let her in
But that is a big if and that's a long when
With all that said I know it wont last
Because I lead with my emotions but I've learned from the past
Still a nice guy that's always me
But if I brush you off that's only part if me
I'm sorry for that hope you see where I'm coming from
My hearts incased in armor and it beats to a new drum
Yeah I'm a playa one day I'll hang it up
Hey it might be tomorrow when that special girl shows up
But until that time I'm taking orders like a waita
So you know how we do, play on playa

© 2007 Dennis M. Stanfield

Still a Playa

Said I'd hang it up when that girl came along
Didn't really believe it but I was wrong
She burst on the scene like sun through the blinds
She is a breath of fresh air, one of a kind
I can't find a flaw in her game
I smile at the mention of her name
Feels like we knew each other in another life
It feels so right…maybe wife?
Nah, not this playa kid
But these quick feelings got me hypnotized like Big
I can't pass it by
Hey this feeling could take me to the sky
I'm still a playa just not a free agent
I'm on a winning team and I know people hate it
She'll tell ya no one can harm me
Because I'm her King and a one man army
She's one of few who can handle my charm
And she wont milk me like a cow on a farm
She got my back
Nothing wrong with that
She's a friend and so much more
Keeping up with her isn't a terrible chore
They say show deep love for a guy
And inside that guy the playa will die
Man I may have found the one I was looking for with out looking
So now we can walk together without looking
Yup she's my copilot on life's journey
Still a playa? Nah, I'm hanging up the jersey

The Man

I'm the man
If I want I can have the world in my hands
Been the man so long my game is rusty
But don't push me I still hush-puppies
Ahh man the nerve of me huh
But I'm all about where I'm from
Forget Diddy I can make you a star
Don't doubt me you can go very far
Trust me you need me in your life
I can light you up and give you some spice
I'm the one your moms told you to look for
And keep him, don't let him walk out that door
Yessirr I can upgrade you
I can give a new swag to you
What more can I say
A gift has been given to you today
Don't worry, I'm humble homes
I'm just giving you my arrogant poem
Lol

The Flyest

She's the flyest chick I've ever seen
Her smile reminded me of a great dream
I mean she could walk into a room and light it up
Like the beams of the new Benz truck
Her fashion is on point
And them shoes…she rocking them joints
A whiff of her fragrance is like wow
You'll be looking at the clouds with out looking down
Have ya head going round and round
She's the Angel of all Angels
She has canaries for her halos
She is the one if ever there was one
So nice she'll have you talking dumb
Man her game is soo right
Try hard but you'll fumble your words despite
Put your best button up on with the right spray
Impress the girl with the color complexion of hay
If you play it right it could be your day
Dog if you get her every one will be jealous
They'll be all over you like a tight shirt from Perry Ellis
What she got covering her body?
Business look, grown women, tight skirt either way she's a hottie
But what makes her the flyest of all is not her look
Its her mind set and belief in the good Book
She knows she hot yet wont take advantage of it
Wow! You got to love it
To get with her you got to be righteous
Now you know why she's the flyest!

© 2007 Dennis M. Stanfield

Seduction

The way she licks her lips
The way she shakes her hips
The brightness of her smile
The way she dresses, her style
She's seductive yet classy
She's sexy and sassy
She is so sick its crazy
Even for a check up the Doc gets hazy
She'll rock ya world with out laying a finger on you
She's so hot girls want her too
Ok ok a little too much
But wait till you feel her touch
We'll not her but someone like her
You can go through life, then find her and ya past is a blur
If you had cancer she'd be the curve
God couldn't have made a better breed of woman
Got me singing love songs, well I can't sing so I'm humming
The seduction is getting out of hand
I can't get her out my mind, I wish she'd come to the Land
But to seduce she would lead me astray
But I'm willing to see her everyday
She seduced me to fall for her love
An Angel sent from above
But wait I had my game on also
To get a boss you got to be a boss too yo
Because I seduced her too

Glamorous

You know what I see?... not the bright lights
But for you, I still see a glamorous life
Yeah. Look at you, young, beautiful, smart
To see you successful it isn't that hard
Treat your self like a queen now, why wouldn't they later?
Anyone who thinks other wise, hater
You have so much love that people don't see
And you know you can be what ever you want to be
The glow in her smile is special, glamorous
And to be in her circle all she asks is trust
Trust, you'll be happy to know her
And basically to know her, is to love her
Love she'll give back to you
You can tell she's special even from my view
Coco butter skin great smile
Drive of an adult but innocence of a child
To be glamorous is to have elegance and charm, plus be hot
Well... I guess that sums up my best friend K. Scott

© 2007 Dennis M. Stanfield

Wings of B

Think of a **B**
Small but has strong wings
Beautiful in color
But don't mess with her
Watching that **B** work is like poetry
Poetry in every wing flap
To write you have to **B** passionate
Or the people won't respect it
To write you have to **B** you
Because only you can **B** you
And you're different, like every **B** is
And who you are and what you're about is what really matters
The glow in your eyes can **B** seen through your fingers
And how they articulate on paper and screen
Your potential can **B** seen and read
Your swagger of a thug
But drive of one whom already has it all
So kind and sweet is she
Known by one letter, **B**
But she also inspirers me
To try and take it to the next level
To **B** all I can **B**
But she
Writes with passion
That's the only way to **B**…
…To me
Sky is not the limit, only a new level
For the strong wings of a **B**
And strong wings has she

Just a Poem

A poem is just a poem
Unless it touches a person, hits home
It can be inspiration to raise a tilted head
It can wake up the seemingly dead
A poem can express feelings felt by many
But until they read it, they felt empty
A poem can be an outlet of words that couldn't be spoken
The tone can be serious or just joking
Put a big smile on your face or make you drop a tear
Give you joy and even take away fear
Long or short, doesn't matter
Random, reckless or following a pattern
Poems are expressions of emotions on paper
There is more between the lines than empty paper
Lives are lived in just minutes in a world you didn't know was there
Flying through clouds way in the air
Poems are a reflection of life
Only through a poem can you live twice
You can find and loose love over and over
Fall in love at first sight and never know her
Dreams come true in poetry
I can be the exact opposite of me
I can say things I usually wouldn't
Things I may not have a chance to say or couldn't
So a poem is not just a poem
It depends on how it hits your dome
What frame of mind you're in
Didn't know your whole life could be captured in a page so thin?

© 2007 Dennis M. Stanfield

Home

She was always there even though she didn't raise me alone
I always felt her even in my home away from home
I always was close being in the Mid-West
She taught me to stand up straight and poke out my chest
Sometime I only saw her in the summer months
One time I saw every weekend of a month
She taught me to be tough and gave me a swag
I hate the way people treat her now, man it got bad
They say she run down and dirty
They don't see her inner beauty, they aren't worthy
Even Jesus took a prostitute in
And when her eyes light up like downtown they want in
When I'm through here I'm a go back and check on her
It's been soo long the time seems like a blur
Being here I feel behind enemy lines almost
But I get treated pretty good, this lady a nice host
But I could never forget my 1st she showed me a new love
She something different to you but she's the D to us
And if you don't know by now
I'm talking about Mo Town

© 2007 Dennis M. Stanfield

Part 4

STORIES

My Mind

Man there's this girl I know
But every time I see her she has to go
She sees me and winks
So I start to follow, but she's gone when I blink
I'm going crazy, I may need a shrink
I try and tell my boys but they pay me no attention
Man, look at her lip gloss just glisten
She gives me that finger that says follow me
I follow round the corner, where is she?
Body type, if I told you, you wouldn't believe me
She has already stolen my heart like a thief
But if she only knew it was hers to keep
Every where I turn I see her but can't touch her
Like she's on TV and my set has a blur
And now I realize why she's so hard to find
Because she only lives through the neurons firing in my mind

© 2007 Dennis M. Stanfield

Diamond Rose

Call your phone your girl pick up
She say, "It's over dude give up"
You was my soul and support like a good shoe
Baby God forgave me so should you
I know I messed up a little bit
Now it's hard to read you like I'm illiterate
I'm a slave to my heart and emotions
And my tears could fill the ocean
Cry? That's what a man isn't suppose to do
Who ever believes that is a damn fool
Her love gives me a rush
And once again I feel like a kid with a crush
Wish I could take it back because now you're gone
It all makes sense now when I hear them love songs
While I'm trying to holla at this flawed diamond shawty
I messed around and let my yellow diamond get cloudy
I got bloody knees praying to Big Homie
I see I didn't handle my business like Jody
Told you I wasn't like other dudes you see
And you just said "Yeah, show me!"
I hurt like an old lady with corns
When you miss handle a Rose you get the thorns
My vision is dark and goes out
I look up in a nervous shout
Girls says "Are you ok? You seem…"
Thank you Big Homie, it was just a dream
He was showing me I was blocking my blessing
I can't give up a lifetime of love for a night of sexing
Ran home to my baby
Told her I was going crazy
She didn't know if she could deal with me
But that's when I asked her to marry me

Play'd

It's usually thought that guys are players
But don't put it past these girls don't give them no favors
Truth be told they do it the best
Try yo girl…put her to the test
Boy O boy women got the world in they hands
Down fall? They'll fight they best friend over a man
But hey I'm not here to debate
Just want to get my story straight
This girl was so good I can't even be mad
To good to be true like she came from a dream I had
She played her role well, shy yet sexy
Like she was innocent but her eyes hexed me
Yo she catered to my ego
Had me at ease like shooting a free throw
Dudes was all over her but she only wanted me
Stop calling all my girls for this one thick like a tree, lol
We had a class together, started sitting close
Study buddies, heat in our eyes could cook a roast
Now I think about it I never saw her outside school
I began to realize I was a fool
Now how real is that?
After the semester she wouldn't call me back
Ain't that some thing, I just got play'd
And it wasn't for a dude, rather a stupid grade
She didn't have to lead me on….

Unknown

I've never even seen her face
But mention her name and I rise with haste
I'm in love with a woman whose features I don't know
And my heart is leading me, telling me where to go
Most likely that's the best way
Because my heart is blind so it can find a needle in the hay
My heart can't discriminate, but it knows what works
It's when "I" get in the way that makes my heart hurt
In my eyes I'm in love with a shadow it seems
Feature that can't be seen even under high beams
But her voice is so fresh, my ear drums dance
Am I going crazy? Am I in a trance?
I can't feel her lips or hug, but my senses are insane
It's like those signals are getting lost on the way back to the brain
I can't even see an outline, like she doesn't exist
It has got to be a catch, got to be a twist
How do I know so much about her, but couldn't pick her out the crowd
I'll just have to go on faith, like that of a child
And that's when I found out I was really in love
Because she turned out more beautiful than I ever could've thought of

The Well

She had my heart in one hand and in the other my pride
And with out pride from the world I couldn't hide
She said choose one or the other
With out my pride I figured I wasn't strong enough to love her
She threw my pride in the well and I jumped in after it
But with out thinking of the aftermath of it
This well was never ending, it went forever
All my thoughts came together, choppy like a blender
Finally I hit the bottom, thought I was done
Pride in my hand, thinking what have I done
I chose pride over my heart, over love
I want to move but I can't I'm a slug
Every bone I have is broken
Now I feel like her heart feels, broken
I pray to God, "Give me one chance"
"To take care of Your angel, her life I'll enhance"
Nothing happen, so fat tears fell from my face
Lying at the bottom of the well, I fell from grace
I closed my eyes and with my last breath
Told God I loved her and prayed for her good health
Then I heard a voice, a familiar one
I thought it was God and Jesus had come
It was her, and she was yelling at me
Telling me how stupid I was, "How dumb can you be"
The light began to fade, then a splash
She threw my heart down, like trash
My heart said to me, "I need to be with her, find a way"
So I made a vow, to start this day
I grabbed my heart and began to climb
I thought of her face, with eyes so kind
I yelled to her, I don't know how
I needed to get to her; she needed to hear me out
I got out the well and spoke to her heart
I wanted her to have mine, I couldn't handle my heart
It should be with the love of my life, with the rising of the sun
My heart with hers, now we could be one
I found "myself" down in that well
I left my pride locked in that cell
So I have to thank God for using that well to save me
And also for the Angel He gave me

I Don't Know You

Who is this dude pushing up on my lady?
I don't know him but I've seen him a lot lately
He looks so familiar; I can't put my finger on it
I got to get him away, got to use my wit
Is he from her past?
A long relationship that didn't last?
These are some things I need to know
I'll get some one to check him out, a pro
Follow him around and see where he goes
How could she do this? I loved her
She's walking and laughing with him, our past seems a blur
But as we follow them more, happiness is only on the surface
Like a terrible hand that you can't hide cause you're nervous
He treats her so wrong
And she's put up with it for so long
I'm better than him. Why did she leave in the 1st place?
To see her now, her pops would yell in her face
This dude has no respect for her and she's lost hope
Something is missing, she feels like an empty stamped envelope
If she only knew I would treat her like a Queen
Like an Angel, a supreme being
Give her what ever she needs, any thing
He leaves her and kisses other females
He even kicks it with the chick that's doing her nails
Enough is enough I've got to intervene
But her and him I can't come between
Now I see this dudes complete history
And he no longer is a complete mystery
I can't come between he and she
Because he is me
Now my heart is beating fast like a drum
Man…. Is this what I've become?

The Fight

It's a fair fight
Both same size weight and height
This type fight does happen often
Except no paper view and fans, lets get it popping
No pads or gloves its to the death
Listen….one of them just took they last breath
How did it come to this you ask?
Well you'll have to go deep, deep into their past
One of them would die before they swallowed pride
They got into it many times before but they let it slide
They collided like two trains on the same track
Two different and they each thought the other was whack
It was a battle like Jay and Nas
City was to small for two gods
One was nice guy the other had a thug mentality
Now you see why they couldn't live happily
Left right shots to the body
Once they even fought over a hottie
But this is different it's the last stand
This is to the end and who's gone be the man?
This a fight for the soul
To win mentally is the goal
You gone be the man ya momma raised you to be?
Or are you gone be the stereotypical black man playa we see?
Stress of this could loose ones health
But its crazy this whole time I been fighting with my self!

Choice

Phone rings as I pop up to look
I had fallen asleep with my business book
Come on Den we got to make a move
This kid around the block we got to get this dude
See I'm the kid with a bright future if I flick the switch
But I'm sitting in the dark and I can't be a snitch
Because in they eyes you got to be down to ride
And if you don't you a punk, go hide
But the money is good and I needs
Helps me to support my momma's kids
They pick me up out back
Everyone in all black
Black SUV man this isn't wise
I'm thinking to myself what am I doing with this guys
We get to the spot, hop out and it's about to go down here
Gun in my hand, I could drown from fear
Their going down a path I don't want to follow
They kick in the door; I take a deep breath and swallow
Couple shots then complete silence
This what I be talking about, black violence
"Den come get some," I don't even know this kid
Man up dude, this is the life we live
All because dude lived on a different block
Things they did I couldn't watch
I find the nerve to speak up
Yo man let's be up
Been here too long
Besides being here some thing else is wrong
Look out the window, flashing lights
I'm already thinking about my rights
Now cats running like roaches
As the SWAT team approaches
Tension too thick for my mind to cut threw
Some one yelling but I can't hear, can't move, I'm stuck in glue
Phone rings, "Den we got to make a move"
Nah I'm good, got studying to do
"Ok college boy get cha next time"
But next time I talked to him he was doing time

American Dream

Look at myself but in a mirror
A little hazy but it gets clearer
Doc is working on me, but why?
I don't know, but they think I might die
How can I be looking at myself like this?
Feel like a ghost but with a twist
See I was following the American Dream
When I should've followed my own dream
Or maybe Malcolm or Martin's dream
But this way of thinking in the hood is a common theme
Bet you didn't know the government ran through the hood in a UPS truck
But all they was dropping off was bad luck
Now I'm trying to avoid a sentence like a bad grammar student
When looking at a paragraph who wouldn't?
Just to catch y'all on
Let ya know where my minds gone
Paragraph is 3-5 times four equals 12-20
20 years just for being black and witty
Now a days dudes are faker than ball head girls in wigs
And to get them by, you'll do illegal gigs
They laughing while we trying harder
Racism still around, they just run it through a purifier and bottle it up like water
The prettiest people are doing the ugliest things
For the pursuit of happiness, the American Dream
Now I'm on this table looking death in the face
Because I was in the way of some ones race
They hunger was stronger than mine
My best friend stabbed me from behind
Dudes from the hood get money and don't know what to do
We doing the government a favor killing each other too
That color green can make one blind
Now my story ends, flat line

Roses

Every night he goes to sleep with roses in his hand
He hopes she will find her way to them
He stayed late at basketball practice and she walked home
Problem was she never made it home
So now he dreams with a broken heart like John Mayer
And searches his dreams for her cause he is his biggest hater
He blames himself and won't give up
But he is killing himself slow, like the burning of a blunt
He has to forgive himself to find his way to her
That's the wall that's blocking him from her
And every day he wakes with roses in his hand and pain in his heart
So he prays to God and says that waking up is the hardest part
God tells the man it was her time, her earthly walk had been complete
Still missing her, but with a better understanding, he rose to his feet
And that night he went to sleep with roses in his hand cut perfectly from the stem
And the next morning, he woke with out them

Part 5

POLITICAL/SOCIAL

Pro Black

Never fired a gun in my life but to protect my fam I'll learn
That thought alone could burn me like a bad perm
The government only sees what they created, the stereotype
They say they don't but P.E. taught me don't believe that hype
I've seen what the government can do and how they be
Yeah they'll help you except its different rules with you and me
Ain't any ports and boats owned by blacks
So how you think we get all this crack
The government distributed it through out the ghetto
Now they sit back like they've got on a halo
They got the cure for disease they got it for AIDS
But the reason poor blacks wont get it is because the government trying to get paid
I'm considered a threat because of my skin
Police the biggest legal gang so of course they gone win
They want to rebuild the hood but the core is broken
We've been praying for a change sitting back and hoping
Black people come together that would scare those at the top
Then we can get our revenge for them selling us that rock
Oprah with a million dollars can build homes in New Orleans
But the government with 10 can't buy a f***ing canteen
Only because blacks and poor whites were the victims
Now they try and play it out like a bad sitcom
I'm still gone throw my fist up and fight till I'm dead
Because a change gone come like Sam Cook said
If you can't respect that ya whole perspective is whack
I'm not anti-white…I'm just Pro Black

© 2007 Dennis M. Stanfield

Still Pro Black

I'm still a threat like a gun tucked in the holster
My face is on a wanted poster
It's all black with no features because a
I'm them I'm they I rep every black face in America
Don't worry I'm working out so I can carry ya
Still don't like the government whole hearted plus a half
Want to burn my flag but can't afford the gas
They say life is a trick only because they want her pants
Respect her and she'll welcome you with open hands
God please help me and my people
Because in Your eyes all people are equal
The government wants to deny You
Most likely because Your skin was the color of Yoo-Hoo
Bad leaders go back to the start of this nation
They almost destroyed the Native persuasion
They gave the red man craps and gambling machines
And the blacks crack guns and things
But with God I can handle what being black in America means
I'm a continue to prove stereotypes wrong
Till I'm dead buried and gone
So I'm still gone vote
Because in my little brothers eyes I see hope
And like heroine that's dope
So I thank God for the Dove
This was just some random thoughts I was thinking of
Hope you can respect that
I'm not anti-white I'm just still Pro Black

© 2007 Dennis M. Stanfield

Y'all Don't Hear Me

You may be listening but you don't hear me though
Little girls in our backyards is getting raped
But you rather buy some Bapes
Y'all don't hear me though
I'm just chilling trying to stack my money
Because I want to chill at home oh I'm acting funny?
Y'all don't hear me though
Sorry I got a girl, but your comment was nice
Nah, I'm good I don't need a little spice
I know what your doing I wasn't born yesterday
Oh now because I don't want to sleep with you I'm gay?
Y'all don't hear me though
Dog because I respect women I'm soft?
Don't be mad when you need tests after the Doc says turn and cough
Y'all don't hear me though
Drug dealers idolized
The government pushing lies
The people are hypnotized
Y'all don't hear me though
Words can hurt just like sticks and stones
But remember Jesus was stoned before He reached the throne
Y'all don't hear me though
The government cares more for the "country" then the people
They take care of the money makers so we'll never be equal
Saw New York, hope we don't have a sequel
Y'all don't hear me though
The people shouldn't fear the government only see them as equals
Rather the government should fear the power of the people
Y'all don't hear me though
They trying to make God disappear like Fred Durst
But I say keep Him 1st
Y'all don't hear me though
Yeah you may be listening but you don't hear me though

© 2007 Dennis M. Stanfield

Paint Brush

We ain't anything but gangsters and thugs
But we weren't the ones who introduced drugs
When you're an artist in the hood with your back to the wall
What you suppose to do when they force ya hand, draw
Strokes of black and grey
Back and forth like that of a good play
But that's over looked do to the violence
Want to be king of the hood, that don't give you divineness
People don't like hip-hop because of the sex, money, and drugs
But what about the ones giving out verbal hugs?
We have to find an identity to better our culture
And leave the next generation with substance and culture
Or else these words will just float in the air
In one ear and out the other ear
We know the stereotypes they paint us as
But it's up to us to put it to rest in the past
So I don't have a pen I have a paint brush
To try and change the picture that they paint us

Mental Stimulation

Let me stimulate your mind for a sec
Put on my shades so you can see through my specs
It's play hard or go home in my rec
Life isn't all bling bling
In that pursuit you'll end up behind bars and screens
The system is already against us
So playing into their hands is senseless
Idolizing thugs and gangstas
If you aren't then you considered a wanksta
What else can you do when you set up to fail
Moms can't move out the projects because she saving for bail
They call it America, most others call it hell
Bet you didn't know Time Warner was run by a black man
American Express is run by a black man
I found out I thought to myself damn
Maybe I don't have to be Jay or Diddy
I don't have to be illegal to move out the inner city
As a black man either way is tough
Getting passed over and discriminated is rough
But I can come back from that unlike being shot for stupid stuff
As many succeed there is more that don't
But until you die don't give up hope
Life is real, it's really no joke
For your brain I just want to give a little poke
Black politicians get no respect
Maybe because they puppets for the rednecks
They got to fight more, can't just settle
Go hard, foot on the gas petal
Malcolm and Martin gave they lives
They were covered in honey walking through the bee hive
Don't just get out and vote, because it's the lesser of two evils
But we should know what the government is doing to our people
Just think about that and go on with your day
Hopefully you'll think different about what you do and say
Really not some thing you wanted to hear
But stimulate ya mind and think more clear

© 2007 Dennis M. Stanfield

Leader

Black people we need a leader
Not exactly Martin or Malcolm
But someone to flip our situation and change the outcome
Someone to articulate the things we stated
Street smart but well educated
From where we are and make it in the corporate world like Jay-Z
But still black power like Mos and Kweli
Someone to be a new voice like Lupe Fiasco
Not alone, run with a crew of real people like the Roots band yo
To represent all blacks, the minority and oppressed
Someone to just speak they mind like Kanye West
This leader wont be the lesser of two evils like the President
This leader will be touched by God and heaven sent
And for the people the leader will represent
Don't matter about male/female just a leader
To take up the struggle for the people and be a teacher
If you reading this now one thing is true
The leader I speak of could be inside you

Dream Come Tru

I to have a dream
When ever I think about it my eyes light up like high beams
But it's so hard to get to, or so it seems
But the black family and community is poor
So trying to maintain middle class is a chore
There are exceptions to every rule
But some of those who make it play the rest as fools
My dream is not to live check to check
Help my parents pay off bills and college, get them out of debt
You see the Government and IRS show us no respect
They say the government going in debt because of welfare
Mean while Canada has free Medicare
On the poor the rich is peeing
Mean while the oil owners is eating
Never hear me blame the white man, not him
Because it's the power, the government, I blame them
But they are mostly made up of old white men
So in a round about way I could blame them
The whole government system is corrupt
And they feed the public the truth slow like syrup
My dream is not to be judged because of my color
And for blacks to stop killing each other
We need a good leader with a great scheme
That could work for my dream
It seems Dr. King's dream dried up quick like morning dew
But when the day comes it'll be a dream come true

Around My Way

Around my way all you really see is crime
Trying to make a dollar out of 15 cents and don't have a dime
Heroes is drug dealers, entertainers, rappers and ball players
Hard to move up because of the haters
What about the blue collar man?
This role model is sinking in the sand
Cats roll through on 20s with doors open wide
But they live with they moms, that's success right?
Rather have my own spot and ride on factory rims
I still get my build on like a dude in construction Tims
Sometimes I look at my hood and feel like a sucker
I mean look around this sucker
It's run down and poverty is crazy
After the Civil Rights my people done got lazy
Seems like MLK's vision of a dream is hazy
Want to blame the government because the hood has gone to Hates
Got a right too because they feed us crack like Gerber Babies
Drugs and murder have ripped my community
What ever happen to the thought of unity?
Just because we got civil rights the fights not over
Look around nights is getting colder
I see potential, but the kids need a chance
They can do more than hold guns in their pants
My ladies is more than a big booty on stage
We can write our own history and turn that page
I know it seems like the hood is a cage
But I'm trying to open your mind as if it was hit by a 12gage
The government won't let us get right with out a fight
Trying to keep us cut off like a pipe
They gone keep feeding us crap and covering it with welfare
That stinks and that crap isn't fair
My people got to stop killing each other today
If we don't the government wins and it's our people who pay
I'm not given in so catch me Around My Way!!

© 2007 Dennis M. Stanfield

If and Might

If I wasn't such a good kid I might run in your house
Or maybe be a player and flirt with your spouse
If I wasn't raised right I might be recruiting your kids
And turning them into thugs that get lifetime bids
If I wasn't in love I might cheat on my girl
Tell her I love her and sleep with the world
If I wasn't a momma's boy I might disrespect your daughter
Use her then toss her like a bottle of water
If I wasn't a big brother I might be running the streets
And calling do gooders, losers and geeks
If I wasn't God fearing I might go against the grain
Do some thing terrible to cause my mom all sorts of pain
If I didn't know a real father I might be a dad
Having a couple different kids and never be the pops they should have
There are a lot ifs and might's in life
But I can only control the inside cabin, not the weather during the flight

Part 6

PERSONAL

Where I Stand

Where I Stand is important to who I am
Rather then sit I'll Stand up for the black vote
I'm a laid back dude and I don't really Stand out
But when I'm needed I try to Stand in
To protect my closest I'll Stand in front
But if they want I'll Stand behind to watch they back
And when you really need me I'll Stand beside you
Got to keep it moving to succeed so I'll never Stand down
Keep pushing forward, not one of these dudes just Standing round
I know I'm short but through it all I try and Stand tall
In today's world you can't just Stand by
Because while you Standing by, life is passing you by
Take a Stand for something….anything
Where do you Stand?

Spaceship

Some time I wish I had a spaceship to fly away
Fly past all my problems straight up into the sky today
Quit this job dude told me I'd never work there again
It's cool for me that was a win win
Man I've been working this grave shift
Schools like another job but I won't stop, not a little bit
Wake up and go to school then work then study
They keep telling me later its gone turn out lovely
My grind and situation is a different kind of struggle
I won't knock yours so don't knock my hustle
Black man in America it's already hart to succeed
But I won't it so bad it's almost a greed
I can't let it get that way
Everyday to me now is a new day
A new day to do something I didn't the day before
I can't keep looking at life like a chore
There are still times I want my ship
Go up to the Milky Way and take a dip
Knock on God's door and ask for Tommie Lee to come out
I can tell him my problems and ask how the Tigers will turn out
Then return to a struggle that may not be so bad
Money helps but it isn't everything...what if I didn't have a dad?
So with all the positives I can't think negative
Because in retrospect...it's all relative
So when I grind and be successful it'll be worth it
I got to wake up everyday like it's on purpose
Life won't be a struggle and problems will be less after that day
Because God will send me a spaceship to fly away
Long as I stay out my own way

© 2007 Dennis M. Stanfield

The Nice Guy Box

So I guess I'm in the nice guy box
For me personally, it's not a bad box
But I'm usually the underestimated dude
Or looked at different if I catch an attitude
I guess you just have to scream and shout all the time
But if I do get loud with you, I'm lying
So I'm acting now, when I'm just being me
I don't have to be a thug to stand up for my girl or me
There is more than one level to a real man you see
No need to fight, for bull crap my skin is thick
But if you get under it, it can get crappy quick
But why?
Am I less of a man cause I let it fly?
Come on man, the world is changing
Rappers are in corporate America and maintaining
Save ya mean mug frown for the mirror
Look beyond your self to see much clearer
You not hard cause you a thug, being a thug is a choice
How proud are you when you not around to hear ya daughters voice
I didn't walk down that road, I chose another
But I still get stereotyped cause of my color
I live in the hood, but I'm not "of" the hood kid
I'm a soft guy because I didn't do a bid?
I'm a nice guy, so…
I'm not You, but I bet I'm a real man though
Probably more real than you
You a coward, man who knew
So why I got to be in a box, why?
Nice guy. Why can't I just be a guy?
Street cred, that's overrated
Fighting because some one said you soft is out dated
Black men not taking care of they're wife and kids, I hate it
So you can call me soft, I'll stay humble
But when ya hard, tough guy self gets hit, I'll laugh when you crumble
So if you're looking to find me, I'll be in my box

© 2007 Dennis M. Stanfield

To Whom It May Concern

To Whom It May Concern
Just fill in the blank when it's your turn
Ever been in love and wanted to make more out of life
Fill like you can rise to the highest heights
To me love is deceitful and success is fictional
Like things that go on, on TV shows
I want to be a millionaire, man I'd take a G
To get things I want and take care of my family
Love is real but there is no perfect mate
In jail 27 sum odd years and divorce was Mandela's fate
America doesn't value these things
Even the King of Pop gave out a ring
On TV they show who wants to marry a millionaire
And the bachelor, man who cares
Most marriages don't last
To get to the top blacks still got to kiss brass
Not enough fathers but a bunch of dads
Too many drug dealers and not enough grads
If you're not ready for love don't open the doo(r)
If you can't be a man for ya girl then let her go
Better to have loved and lost then never to have loved
Only if it makes you a better person and you've learned from love
Don't let them get you down success is yours to take
But you got to want it and be ready because they want you to break
Try to find God and take his hand
Sincerely Dennis, a flawed man

Questions?

Why do people still question me?
Some people just wont let me be
Questioning my motives and choices
When I make a decision its like I hear voices
I don't question people on what they do even if suspect
If asked I give advise but don't look at them different none the less
I'm not trying to make any one happy but myself
Because trying to please people will lead to bad health
So now I'm playing post man and addressing questions!
Don't take it wrong I'm not threatening
Before I make some one else happy I have to make myself happy see
No one will respect me if I don't take care of me
Some time the kid just wants to chill and get his life on track
To some that may seem whack
But I'm 22 now and not getting younger
I'm not gone hold back and be a fronter
If you can't add to my life fall back
Because if my friends have no goals or morals then those also I will lack
I got goals to obtain and a future to plan
With God behind me I can hold my future in my hand
I'm pretty good at hiding how I feel
Only because I don't want everyone going through my ordeal
So in that I keep to myself inside my own head
In that I feel comfort like the perfect bed
I'm a man who leads with his emotions
And I got a big enough heart to fill the ocean
But some times that's not enough to please people
I'm not gone rush to every call, that's not equal
Got a new girl but not to replace any one
She made her own band and is beating her own drum
She's not like the other girls not to take away from them
They were all different, that's why I liked them
And she brings a new chapter to my life style
And reading this book so far is worth wild
We can enjoy the simple things at will
Little, like going to the park to chill
People not gone want us to make it
But we closer because of that and they hating it
Just getting life off my chest
No disrespect
Just my next direction
Now any questions?

© 2007 Dennis M. Stanfield

Void

The man, the myth, the legend
Was taken from me and is now in Heaven
In my life now there is a void
My heart was infiltrated like the walls of Troy
Hopped out the horse and my heart was destroyed
Yeah I should be happy I had him for 20years
But that still doesn't help at night with the fears
I want him for 20 more, he was a light
And in my life that light shinned bright
Now my happiness is only temporary
Seems that search is only arbitrary
On this journey I feel alone
Looking for him to guide me home
I lost my grandfather in Nov. of 04
And now to maintain happiness is a chore
I always tried to play it off like I was cool
Because I wanted no one else to feel my blues
That sits on mostly ladies in my life
So in that case its hard to really call one my wife
I would love for it to happen but I doubt
I still love to love and love everything loves about
To maintain a relationship has been kind of strange
Because there's a void and not to be hurt is my aim
To everyone I affect I say sorry to you
But it is what it is and the void I'm fighting through

I Live Down Here

It will be three years in November
I can see him now laughing and standing tall in his entire splendor
I miss him everyday
To get him back what wouldn't I pay
But God called him right?
To send him a message I need a lot of string and a big kite
Or maybe a spaceship flight
He's living in the sky, higher
Still can't understand why as I get wiser
Still remember a joke he told that never gets old over time
Put his big finger close to my face, makes me laugh every time
"I live down here, you live up there, come down and see me some time"
I would laugh so hard as he ran his finger from my forehead to my chin
Never on a kids face have you seen such a grin
He would then grab me and put me on his knee and say hold on
That is before I got too big and grown
He once told me I couldn't drive or have a girl till I was 23 or 25
Man oh man I wish he was still alive
To see me graduate and make a beautiful women my wife
Or tell me more things about my dad, my dad wouldn't like
Ah, I feel an empty space in my life
I miss him saying grace at our Thanksgiving feast
But I feel his presence every time a wind blows from the East
And he lives in me and I'll never forget
And I know he's up there in Jesus' private tent
Big Homie take care of him for all time
Hey granddad, I live down here, you live up there, come down and see me some time….

1980 Sumin

April 25, 1984 from a Queen goddess a young King was born
The angel that delivered him from God made it through the storm
The look from her eyes to his was so warm
Still too early to call out his future though
Trying to walk in the footsteps left for him, there's hope
I've grown, 22 years strong
Still learning and deciphering right from wrong
Looking to settle down into my thrown
Hoping to take care of that Queen before she's gone
Looking for a new Queen
Hold your horses there is a difference between
One brought me in and the other will bring in
Bring our future Kings & Queens into a world of sin
But what I've learned since the 80s I'll use
Use to mold them and help with the decisions they choose
1980 sumin, but the book isn't finish
Yes I got a lot more winnas (winters)
Pardon my slang
Just trying to advance from the 80s in which I came
From the era of the introduction of crack
And don't forget the flyboy the Mack
To the age of the Internet
And more and more terrorist threats
Government still the same
Running things like a game
From Magic, MJ & Bird to Mello, Bron & Wade
Blacks still selling something to get paid
Don't got to get into that
It's a New Era, got to get a new hat
Switching up letters now I'm on JR like a junior
Want JRs later rather than sooner
I'm two decades in the life
Learned a lot from life
Things changed daily, don't believe the hype
Did but never really really considered a wife
But as we grow so does our maturity & mind
And you know what? So has mine
Yo momma I made it!
I'm on my way
From 1980 sumin to today
Yo it's crazy
Shout out to all the 80s babies
I'm just getting started

© 2007 Dennis M. Stanfield

Thank You

Special? Nah this isn't the one
Just a little background then I'm done
I get a lot of complements on my blogs
I appreciate them all, I kind of feel like a frog
That got kissed by a princess and now I'm top dog
I'm just a blessed dude with a gift I guess
Got to thank my Roses like Kanye West
Don't send flowers, my friends send themselves
Yo I got lucky at Wal-Mart, they had a sale
People around me make up who I be
So I thank all y'all for the poems you see
I'm just a reflection of my friends
So the strength of my writing is in their hands
Now my goal is to open up a store for aspiring Art-Tees (artists)
I wont sell you a dream, but the inspiration is free
I'm inspired by the littlest thing you don't understand
A word and a smile could change the face of this land
I'm not famous so I can't do it for fame
I just like speaking what I know, but in my range
It feels good when some one says, "I enjoyed that"
A joy you can't get from smoking crack
To inspire some one, that is fun
But I got to thank God for that one
So I'm a continue to do my best and keep them all fresh
To help myself and y'all release some stress
Good looking out…

© 2007 Dennis M. Stanfield

Thank You's

God, the head of my life. I'm trying!
Mom (L'Tanya) My biggest fan
Dad (Dennis Sr.) My Bar
Mr. and Mrs. Ribbins
Raheem, Demetria and Tommie Lee
My Grandparents (Tommie Sr., Christine)
Momma C
Poppa (Doctor William Childress)
My Uncles
    Alex, Jr., Greg, Ray, Anthony
My Aunties
    Avis, Darice, Sandi, DeShaune, Gene, Cynthia, Diane
My Cousins
    Jessica, Tiffany, Kyla, Tara, Chai, Kiesha, Lauren, Jeramy, Chris
My Fam by state:
    Mansfield, OH (I haven't forgotten y'all!)
    Mississippi
    New York
My Friends
    Jocelynn, my best friend. You're a big inspiration Love!
    Lee, Ben, Pat, Jamie, Dustin, Raychl, Fran, Lex, Michelle, Anica, Briana, Sam & Jon, John B., John R., Te'erra, DeAntye, Keesha, Melissa, Karli(BFF), B(From day one)

I have a lot of family and friends. So to everyone or any one I may have missed; You know how you have impacted my life and I appreciate everyone!

Your name goes here _____!

www.ingramcontent.com/pod-product-compliance
Lightning Source LLC
LaVergne TN
LVHW011430080426
835512LV00005B/355